Positively ✦ Freakin' ✦ Amazing

A 3-MINUTE JOURNAL FOR DITCHING NEGATIVITY AND EMBRACING YOUR FABULOUS AUTHENTIC SELF

Gabby Frost

For anyone who has ever felt so alone in this world that you thought things would be better off without you: You are not alone, and you never will be. But you are also wrong: I am so glad you're here.

creating this book was

POSITIVELY FREAKIN' AMAZING

but also really hard

For years, I've been lightly manifesting the chance to publish my art in some capacity. When that opportunity finally came, I was elated. Little did I know working on this book would also give me a chance to work on myself, as the offer coincided with a phase of personal recovery that came out of left field.

For context, I'd just started a new job and was finally moving out after spending three years back at home due to COVID-19. I'd felt so lost since quarantine started. I broke up with my partner of almost five years one month before lockdown. I became an empty shell of myself. I felt the same on the outside but not inside.

I didn't even realize I was struggling with burnout until I graduated from college in my living room and started my first post-grad job. I began stepping back from GMF Designs (my creative outlet for art, words, and memes) but ultimately became even more burnt out.

Prior to seeking professional intervention, I experienced one of the scariest things for the first time: passive suicidal ideation. Explaining this to my psychiatrist and mother without causing concern was difficult. I have terrible existential anxiety, and my ideation would have me at a point where I felt like no one benefited from my existence. Like, what even was the point? I spent almost a year unemployed because I knew I needed to address my mental and physical health problems in order to live the life I wanted. In December 2021, I received a diagnosis that changed my life: Premenstrual Dysphoric Disorder (PMDD for short).

I started taking Zoloft the day I got diagnosed, and ever since then, my PMDD has been pretty manageable. I went more than a year without having a bad PMDD episode, but while I was concocting this book, I experienced my first very low points in a while. It was nowhere near the severity of the episodes in 2020 and 2021, but it still made me feel like I was failing everyone. My manager and coworkers. The lovely team that helped me make this book. My best friends. I just didn't have the energy to deal with everything.

The only thing pushing me was deadlines, as I heavily struggle with executive functioning (shout-out to ADHD) and procrastination has been my number one enemy/de facto motivator since I was in elementary school.

Yeah, I was that kid who asked their parent to help them with a project I'd known about for weeks the night before it was due. But I always crushed it!

But this was different. I couldn't focus to the best of my ability at work, or on this book or really even do the most basic of things. It wasn't until I spoke up and asked for help from my family, friends and work family that I rose from the ashes. I've always hated asking others for help; it does not come naturally to me at all. But the bottom line was I needed it. And reader, they gave it to me.

People won't know something is a problem for you until you communicate that to them. Keeping your thoughts and feelings to yourself doesn't always give them the space they need to expand so you can process them for what they are. When you see your thoughts and feelings in the light of day (or at night, your call), you can decide which of them are good for you and which ones you can let go.

I'm not ashamed to say I was depressed and anxious while working on something I dreamed of accomplishing. After finally achieving something I'd been working toward for years, I thought I'd be at my happiest. Except I wasn't. That's the way life is sometimes. But writing this book made me realize my purpose again. Toward the end, I started coming out of the depressive episode and felt that same creative fiery passion I did when I started GMF.

I'm so grateful to have people in my life who genuinely care about my growth and success. They've helped me understand that it's OK to make mistakes and slip up; it's not the end of the world and it'll only teach me things. As an example, in my case, if you think you have another learning disorder (dyslexia) on top of your ADHD and don't do well with specific tasks no matter how hard you try, you should tell someone and try to seek accommodations. Your mileage may vary!

As a result of the struggle to finish this book, I also found a renewed sense of self. My purpose is to bring people together, to make others feel like they're loved, supported, validated and safe. That's all I want. I don't want anyone to feel the same awful, dark feelings I experienced at rock bottom without the proper support or care.

This book is for anyone who has ever felt like no one understands how you feel. Although our emotions can be heavy and our inner voice convinces us we're alone, we're not. This is why it's so important to spark conversations on mental health and normalize being human to its full extent.

I hope *Positively Freakin' Amazing* helps you have the tough conversations with yourself that you need to have and gives you the strength to talk to others if that's what you need. I know being self-aware and honest with yourself can be a feat, but it only helps you become the best possible version of yourself.

You got this. I believe in you and always will.

—GABBY

What are the upsides of outgrowing what doesn't suit you anymore? List a few awesome things that happened when you let go of the past.

your trauma is NOT your fault

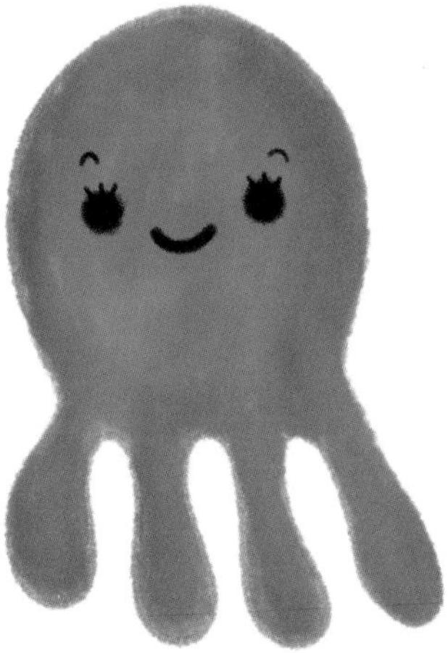

Think of a couple of affirmations to repeat to yourself when your inner thoughts are being little shitheads.

you deserve rest even if you haven't been productive

Just because you have things to do doesn't mean you should put rest on the back burner. Be gentle with yourself and don't spread yourself too thin. What does taking time to pause and refresh look like to you? Write or doodle activities that help you unwind (e.g., reading, going out in nature). Feeling guilty? Put "take a nap" on your to-do list so you can cross it off.

It's easy to feel like you're not worthy of being loved, but when that happens, know that your thoughts are spouting straight-up nonsense. Write or doodle different times your thoughts lied to you and what you said to counter them.

IT'S OK TO TAKE THINGS slow

What is a long-term goal that you
know will take some time to accomplish?
Write or doodle steps you need to take to
eventually reach your goal. Take your time!

you are not a failure because others don't appreciate your worth

You are worthy and you deserve to believe that. Write down or doodle five things you like about yourself. Keep them in your back pocket.

HEALING DOESN'T HAPPEN ALL AT ONCE, AND THAT'S OK.

Healing can be a challenging process, and that's OK. Write down or doodle three to five things you want to heal. Work on them one piece at a time.

it's ok to

feel
confident

celebrate
yourself

establish
boundaries

take mental
health days

stand
up for
yourself

outgrow
other people

Repeating positive affirmations can do wonders on days when you're feeling the worst. Write down six affirmations (with doodles?) you want to repeat to yourself more often.

YOUNGER YOU WOULD BE SO PROUD

Describe something that would make younger you proud of current you. It can be big or small—all accomplishments are important.

your problems matter, whether they're big or small

Regardless of the relative scope of
the issues you're facing, they matter to you!
Write about ways you can cope in a
healthy way during stressful situations.

REMINDER:
you are
enough
as you are!

You'll always be enough as you are—I promise. Describe some non-physical traits you like about yourself. You matter, inside and out.

YOU ARE doing just FINE

Think about something you're currently working on. It can be anything, even keeping most of your houseplants alive. What progress have you made? Take a beat to savor the journey, not just the end goal.

You deserve all the dope stuff that comes your way. How do you celebrate yourself and your accomplishments? Write or doodle your methods below.

it's ok if
others have
it worse
than you,
you still
deserve help!

Suffering isn't a competition—everyone could use some help in their own way, and you don't need to convince anyone that what you're struggling with is a struggle. Period. Write what you wish others told you when you were going through a hard time.

YOU DON'T NEED TO PROVE YOUR TRAUMA TO ANYONE!

You don't need to have others validate your pain or the scars that remain. Ever. It's OK if you don't want to share your trauma publicly. Share the things you want to heal from on this page. Or...don't. Just make a list in your mind.

Burnout is a bitch. Sometimes we need to step back and take time for ourselves in order to feel "normal" again. List the activities that help you go back to feeling like yourself when things are rough.

it's ok to
grow & bloom
into a new
version of you

OLD ME

NEW ME ☺

Out with the old you and in with the new. What are some traits you want to work on and improve? Take up the space you need to level up like the badass you are.

CONGRATS
on all your
accomplishments,
both big
and
small

Write or doodle some of your recent achievements, regardless of their significance in the grand scheme (because they matter to you!). Then go celebrate those wins on your own terms—cake optional.

you are more than
your mental illness
or trauma

You are not the things you've been through.
(Read that again.) Think about the stuff
that makes you *you* and write down
your favorite things about yourself.

Putting
yourself
♥ first ♥
is NOT
selfish

Someone's got to look out for you—and who knows your vulnerabilities better than you? The world does not revolve around you, but your life does. You don't need to people-please and put others' feelings before your own, especially if doing so requires sacrificing your well-being. Write or doodle ways you can put yourself first on a frequent basis. You deserve it!

IT'S OK
TO HAVE A

BAD
MENTAL
HEALTH
DAY

We all have bad days—those moments suck, sure, but just remember: It's part of being human (which is pretty rad overall!) and it's not your fault. Write or doodle a self-care list of things to do on bad mental health days that'll help you get through it.

I wish I could go back and tell younger me that everything will be ok

Hey you. Your younger self is so proud of you—not just of the things you've done, but of the person you've become. Think about some moments or experiences little you would be jumping with joy to hear about and write about them below.

BE PROUD OF YOURSELF IF YOU

got out of bed	brushed your teeth	washed/put away laundry

showered or bathed	cleaned up your room	drank water

OR JUST BREATHED TODAY.
"SIMPLE" ACCOMPLISHMENTS
DESERVE RECOGNITION.

Little tasks can sometimes take a big chunk of energy to check off our to-do lists or seem scarier than they are (especially if you're going through a rough time). But you can do it! Think about a few tiny tasks you can complete this week that you've been putting off. Baby steps!

tending to your mind
and body when they
need you most is
one of the most
beautiful acts
of self-love

physical
health

mental
health

Keeping up with your mental and physical health can sometimes look different—what improves one might not always address the other. But each of your lil health flowers deserves water (aka attention). Create a Venn diagram or write a list of the self-care activities that help with your mental health, physical health or both.

YOUR
FEELINGS
ARE 100%
VALID

It's OK to experience emotions that might not be categorized as "good." You know what else isn't good? Bottling up or burying your feelings. But guess what: Every single feeling you've had today is valid. Write down a few you've experienced today and how you processed them.

IT'S OK TO FAIL OR MAKE MISTAKES

Remember the wise words of Hannah Montana: "Everybody makes mistakes." We all screw up, and that's OK—it's a chance for us to learn and make things right. What matters most is what we do to fix the situation. Write about one of the times you took accountability and bounced back from a mistake, rejection or failure.

take it one

day at a time

When it comes to becoming who you want to be, the length of the journey doesn't matter as long as you are working toward your goal. Sometimes change takes time, and beating yourself up isn't going to make things happen any faster. Write down or doodle what actions you can take on a daily basis to better yourself and your well-being.

WE ALL HAVE MENTAL HEALTH ISSUES

Your experience matters whether you have a mental health diagnosis or not. You have a right to heal from what's hurt you. Write about how you manage your well-being (meditation, medication, working out, etc.) and maintain self-awareness when life gets busy.

my positively freakin' amazing playlist

♡ _____   ♡ _____

♡ _____   ♡ _____

♡ _____   ♡ _____

♡ _____   ♡ _____

♡ _____   ♡ _____

Music often says the words we can't articulate. It can also help us feel better about ourselves. Create a playlist full of music that makes you feel good for a pick-me-up on even the gloomiest days. Describe how each song makes you feel below.

NORMALIZE MENTAL HEALTH DAYS

The brain needs rest and time to unwind just like the body does when you feel unwell or out of sorts. Mental health days should be a necessity, not a privilege. Use the space below to remind yourself of that. Brush away the guilt and take a day off if you need to!

put your well-being first

You deserve to feel good and enjoy life,
and your well-being should be put ahead of
everything else. Speak up and self-advocate!
Write about or doodle the things that
positively impact your well-being,
then make a point to do them this week.

All of us are growing and transforming, whether we're aware of it or not. What are some nostalgic relics that you used to adore? Why did you outgrow them? In what ways do they still bring you joy?

NORMALIZE THERAPY

NORMALIZE MEDICATION

NORMALIZE TALKING ABOUT MENTAL HEALTH

Suffering is a part of the human experience, but you are strong enough to make it through. And you don't have to do it without help. Write or doodle a plan for how you can manage your mental health (e.g., mindfulness, therapy, exercise) for days when you feel out of sorts.

I AM NOT
RESPONSIBLE
FOR THE
VERSION OF
ME THAT
EXISTS IN
YOUR HEAD.

You can't control the way others view you, but guess what? That's not your job (hurray!). Be like Elsa and let that shit go. Turns out the only opinion that matters is your own. Doodle a picture of how you see yourself and what makes you feel unique and special.

friendly reminder

you are worthy of love,
not just from others,
but from yourself too.

Self-love is one of the most important
kinds of love—and you're the only source!
Don't be stingy. It's the longest relationship
you have, so make it count! Create a little
self-love shrine and doodle the parts
of yourself you love the most.

this discomfort
will one day
bring growth

A flower can't bloom without growing in dirt. It's OK to be in uncomfortable situations in life. We can't grow as people without leaving our comfort zone. When have you blossomed beautifully from past uncomfy situations? How can you blossom from a current awkward situation?

it's ok
that you're
changing and
outgrowing
your old self.
you'll be ok.

We may not change as quickly or dramatically as the moon or the seasons, but we all go through different cycles in life. That's nature, baby. Doodle some past versions of yourself and think about what parts of you stood out in that era. (Embrace the cringe! That just means you've grown.)

it's ok to feel
things other
than happiness

How do you cope with your emotions when you feel sad, frustrated, cynical, lonely or unheard? Make a playlist to help you sit with those feelings. Write the songs, albums or artists below.

Say it again for the people in the back: Mental health is health. But the things that affect our emotions and psyche have repercussions for our physical health, too. What are some ways you notice your mental health showing up in your body for better or worse? Write about how you feel. There are no wrong answers.

your
anxious
thoughts
are lying
to you

You're stronger than your anxieties.
But sometimes it's impossible to drown them out.
Write or doodle things you can do to distract
yourself when your anxious thoughts won't
shut their damn mouths (how rude!).

You don't like everyone—no one says you have to! The flip side of this is that it's totally cool if others don't like you. All that matters is that *you* like you. Write or doodle things about yourself that make you, well, you. Whether it's your interests, talents, hobbies or traits, celebrate your favorite parts of yourself —whether they like it or not.

just because you're hurt doesn't mean it's ok for you to hurt other people

Sometimes when we're hurt, we unknowingly hurt others. Doing a mental check-in with yourself to recognize when you're feeling this way can help get you through it and keep you from passing your pain on to those around you. Consider a few of the emotional or physical "warning signs" that you're hurt and write them below.

your trauma
doesn't have
to "<u>teach you
a lesson</u>."

trauma happens
<u>for no reason</u>.

Bad things happen. That's it. That's the tweet. Just because something awful or traumatic happened to you does not mean you deserved it or that you should find a way to see a negative experience in a positive light. You aren't obligated to spin your trauma into something transformative. Write about things that you want and *do* deserve. Manifest the good things that you want to come to you.

you
ARE
capable
OF
★ anything ★
YOU PUT
your mind
★ TO ★

You are capable of anything your mind desires (except getting 1D back together—that'd take a miracle). Think about all the times in the past you doubted yourself but still pulled through. Write about those experiences below.

reminders
⭑ from lil ghost ⭑

you are
worthy

you are
more than
your anxiety

crying
is cool

you
deserve
to rest

you are
one of
a kind

It's reminder time! Bask in a moment of supernatural affirmation from this tiny friend. Write or doodle five reminders your own lil ghost can tell you on days when your thoughts are being scary.

It's ok if
it won't matter
in 5 years, if
something makes
you upset, angry,
overwhelmed or
anxious, you're
allowed to feel
that way!

Feel your feelings. You don't need to bottle them just because it won't matter later. It matters right now, so cry. Scream. Or just let it go. Make sure you're doing whatever you need to do to express yourself and deal with your stressors so you aren't still worrying about it five years down the road. Write or doodle ways you can regulate your emotions.

repeat until you believe it:

I AM ENOUGH and I ALWAYS will be enough. I don't need to prove my worth to anyone!!!

Repeating a positive, empowering message
to yourself can do wonders. Think about what
message your brain needs to hear the most
right now, write it down and repeat
it to yourself until you believe it.

Life moves fast and slow at the same time, and sometimes we end up distancing ourselves from the things that make us feel like us. Think about what things made you happy in the past, then write or doodle what you want to bring back into your life. (You can also write about what you'd rather leave in the past—growth is good!)

Boo to anyone who makes you feel less than for being single. You don't need a significant other to be "whole"—you are complete as you are. Write or doodle ways you can show yourself love.

What makes you feel fulfilled? The thing that gets you out of bed each morning doesn't have to be grand—it could be as simple as enjoying yourself, making someone smile or helping others find their spark. Write or doodle what your purpose means to you.

listen to your body. if it's telling you to take a break, you deserve one.

You know your body better than anyone. If it's telling you to hit the brakes and rest, do it. Get into the habit of taking a break before you're running on empty. Practice writing ways you can let others know you're putting your well-being first so you're prepared next time you need to step away and show yourself some love.

IT'S OK TO TALK ABOUT MENTAL HEALTH

According to the National Institute of
Mental Health, more than one in five people have
a mental illness, but five in five of us have
mental health. Talking to others about how
we're feeling and our lived experiences should
be a normal part of life, not a stigmatized
one. Use this page to write down anything
you haven't told others but want to.

ALL OF YOUR EMOTIONS ARE VALID, EVEN THE "BAD" ONES

Your feelings deserve to be processed,
even the heavy or uncomfortable ones.
Let out those hard thoughts below
in writing or doodles.

your
Mental
Health
is more
IMPORTANT
than any job

There is not a single job that should come before your mental health. You are more than just a number: You are human. What are your red flags when it comes to a job? Define them so you'll know what to watch out for. Then add a few green flags as well, so you know when a job is offering the stuff that you want/need!

Even on your lowest days, when your thoughts start to spiral and it feels like you're barely getting by, you deserve to pat yourself on the back for keeping at it. What are some things you can tell yourself or do for yourself to keep pushing through the toughest moments?

YOU ARE VALID

it's ok if you're feeling uncreative or unproductive

We all have moments of low activity in life. Think of them as your personal winter—it happens once in a while, but it doesn't last forever and it's not inherently bad. Take some time to rest and recharge your brain. Write down or doodle the activities that help you feel rejuvenated when it's time to let yourself hibernate.

Anxiety loves lying to you, but resilience is a bigger badass. Write some statements to help you hold your ground when the "what ifs" come calling.

* you
DON'T
NEED TO
punish
YOURSELF
* FOR WHAT
you eat

You deserve to eat what makes you feel happy without being questioned or harassed. Think about the foods that bring you joy, whether it's a flavor you're obsessed with or a dish or treat that makes you feel nostalgic and sentimental. What do you like about them?

friendly reminder

sharing your feelings is brave. being vulnerable isn't a weakness.

Saying your inner thoughts out loud can be a daunting task, especially when you've grown up thinking it's shameful to do so. Letting loved ones know how you're doing mentally takes courage. What would you share if you felt like you could? (Spoiler alert: I believe in you.)

you have grown oh so beautifully

2 years
ago

last
year

this
year

Growth can seem like a slow process, when viewed through a day-to-day lens. But look back at the past two years and think about how much you've changed. Even when it feels like you're getting nowhere fast, trust the process. Below, list short-term and long-term goals that will help you continue to grow and bloom into the person you want to be.

you are worthy
of the same
love & compassion
you give
others

The kindness you project outward is something you deserve to extend inward, too. It's easy to slip into the role of our own worst critic when we should be our #1 cheerleader. What are some ways you can incorporate being more compassionate toward yourself into your daily routine?

Your worth is not determined by what you accomplish—whether that's for others, e.g., your job, or for yourself, e.g., household chores. You deserve a day off just like everyone else. What are some ways you can relax and refresh that make you feel better?

GIVE YOURSELF
PERMISSION TO
SAY NO!

Sometimes saying no is the best decision you can make to protect your peace. Think of a few times in the last couple months when you could've set boundaries by declining certain things. Describe how you could have said no in those situations.

you make life
worth living

Who brings a smile to your face without fail?
Write down and/or doodle the people you're
grateful to experience life with—whether they're
someone you love platonically or romantically.

the littlest things can
sometimes bring us
the biggest joy

What are the tiny moments that make your heart beat with purpose and bring a genuine smile to your face? Write about them and why they make you feel warm inside.

this is your reminder that you can get through this week. you got this.

Sometimes the only thing that keeps me going is telling myself, "I can get through this week—I just did it the week before, and now I'm doing it again." So in case you need to hear it: Hell yeah, you got this! Write or doodle things that hype you up on your hardest days.

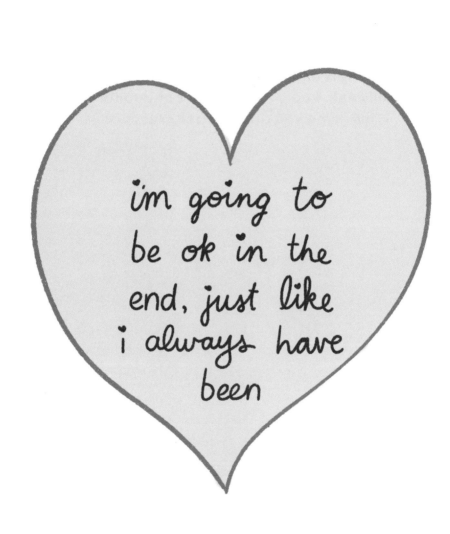

i'm going to be ok in the end, just like i always have been

Think about all the times you've felt nothing but dread, anxiety and hopelessness, but you made it through. Describe those moments below and how you feel about them now that they're firmly in the past. Your perseverance deserves to be celebrated, you unstoppable badass.

you don't have to bottle up your anger

Reflect on how you process and regulate anger. Do you hold it all in until you inevitably erupt like a destructive volcano? Or do you have more healthy ways to unleash it? Describe or doodle your methods below and note where you can make improvements.

It's OK to ask for help when you don't know what to do or need extra support. Reaching out to a trusted friend or medical professional is not only brave but the best way to look out for yourself. Write about what you can say to your support system next time you're at a low point and could use the extra love.

never diminish
your happiness
for the sake
of others

When you're pumped up and excited about something, how do you express happiness? Do you allow yourself the time and space to fully acknowledge your joy? How do you celebrate yourself and your feelings?

you deserve
to surround
yourself with
people who are
good for your
mental health

Community is an important part of the healing process—there's no need to go it alone! Who makes up your main support system? What do your friends do to help you feel supported?

YOU ARE WORTHY

the best memories are the ones we don't realize we're making

There's so much happening all the time, and sometimes that can overwhelm us to the point where we lose sight of our most cherished memories. So take a moment to reclaim them from the chaos. Describe your most treasured moments below.

♡ MY EMOTIONAL SUPPORT MEDIA ♡

MOVIES

TV SHOWS

MUSIC

Most of us have movies, TV shows and music we turn to for comfort. Write about your favorites in each category and all the feel-good, cozy ways they boost your serotonin levels below.

you deserve to
look in the mirror
and love who
you see

We look at ourselves multiple times a day, and we all deserve to love the person staring (or hopefully smiling) back. Affirmations can make mirror time a mood-boosting experience. Jot down a few loving reminders you can repeat to yourself on days when it feels like you don't recognize the person you see in the mirror.

RECOVERY
is not one size fits all

Recovery—much like life—is different for everyone. What works for me might not work for you, and that's OK. For this reason, I left some space for you to write about anything you like. Is there a question you've been pondering that you want to explore?

ways to heal your inner child

- ☐ take up that hobby you always wanted to try
- ☐ watch that show or movie you weren't allowed to see
- ☐ buy the big toy you always wanted
- ☐ dress how you always wanted

Caring for your inner child can bring peace and clarity into your life. Take a moment and think about the things (e.g., activities, clothing, media) you wanted to enjoy as a kid but weren't able to. Create a little inner child bucket list, then go do those things!

you don't need to do everything at once, take it step by step

You can't heal yourself all in one day (and that's not your fault—that's how it is). Making progress involves taking lots of little steps in order to build lasting change. Don't overwhelm yourself by doing too much at once. Take a deep breath and list tiny actions you can take toward your healing goal. There's no competition or clock to beat, so take the time you need.

you don't
need to
post about
your trauma
online for
it to be valid

The things you're dealing with have validity whether the whole world knows about them or not. It's OK if you would rather keep some of your darkest moments to yourself or share them in private with people you trust. Use this page to jot down anything you want to scream out but are opting to keep offline.

block people
who are bad
for your
mental
health

We all deserve to create boundaries both in real life and online. The urge to scroll (and scroll and scroll) is real, but continuously consuming content isn't always what's best for our well-being. Neither are the musings of the trolls we'd be better off blocking. Make a list of your digital boundaries. How can you ensure you're honoring them?

your worth is not defined by

your weight

your likes & followers

your mistakes

Make a list of non-physical things you want to base your worth on (e.g., your compassion, empathy, understanding, showing up for loved ones, spreading kindness). Write down why each of these matters to you and how you'll incorporate all of them into your life.

REMEMBER TO FORGIVE YOURSELF

Things don't always go as planned—sometimes it's out of our control, and sometimes we fall short. Either way, beating yourself up won't fix the matter at hand and it certainly won't make you feel better. What recent flubs or shitty situations have you given yourself a hard time about? List the steps you can take to forgive yourself, accept what's happened and move on in a healthy way.

dear future self,
just know that
i'm proud of
you, just like
i've always
been ♡
love, past self

If you're going to compare yourself to anyone at all, it should be your past self. The only person you should want to be better than is who you were yesterday, not others. Reflect on the ways you've grown and the areas that could still use some work.

YOU'VE FINISHED
THE JOURNAL

Now list everything that's freakin' amazing
about yourself, your life and your world.

_____

_____

_____

_____

_____

_____

_____

_____

_____

_____

_____

_____

_____

ACKNOWLEDGMENTS

First off, a huge thank you goes to you. Without the community we've created together on GMF Designs, this book wouldn't be possible. I know that sounds corny, but it's completely true. Without you all, I wouldn't have the motivation to be genuine and normalize the human experience. I find so much purpose in helping others realize "Hey, I'm not the only one to feel this way" and hope my art helped you in the same way it helped me.

This also wouldn't be possible without my family, who never pushed me away from making a career out of social media. Shout-out to my parents though, as they started the domino effect of all of this by buying me my first laptop (to make up for the fact I was becoming a big sister again at 11).

I could write a whole other book about how much I love my best friends. Thank you Nicole, Taylor, Lauren, Amelia and Steph for being a positive influence on my life and helping me become the best version of myself.

Thank you to some of my mental health art besties too; @burntoutbrain, @crazyheadcomics, @anxiousblackgirlcomics, @selfcarespotlight and @selfcareisforeveryone, I love spreading awareness and normalizing the conversation alongside you all. :)

And of course, last but not least, One Direction.

ABOUT THE AUTHOR

Gabby Frost is a mental health advocate, artist and social media professional based outside Philadelphia. Having established an affinity for digital design and doodling since childhood, she founded GMF Designs in January 2019. She is also the founder of Buddy Project, a mental health nonprofit she started at the age of 15.

Media Lab Books
For inquiries, call 646-449-8614

Copyright 2024 Gabby Frost

Published by Topix Media Lab
14 Wall Street, Suite 3C
New York, NY 10005

Printed in Korea

ISBN-13: 978-1-956403-59-6
ISBN-10: 1-956403-59-0

This journal is not a replacement for professional help or therapy. An important part of loving yourself is realizing when things are too much or when you need help. If you find yourself struggling, please reach out to a mental health professional in your area. Not sure where to start? Consider calling the helpline for the National Alliance on Mental Illness: 800-950-6264, or text "HelpLine" to 62640.

YOU'RE AMAZING! YOU JUST MIGHT NOT KNOW IT YET.

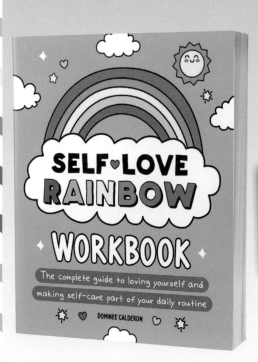

ENCOURAGING AFFIRMATIONS, COLORFUL ILLUSTRATIONS AND MORE!

AVAILABLE WHEREVER BOOKS ARE SOLD